Patricia O. Akinrogunde, Ed.D.

THE Triple Joy
LEADERSHIP JOURNAL: OLIVE JOY FAITH-BASED EDITION

A 90 DAY JOURNEY TO LEAD WITH VISION, COURAGE, AND FAITH

Copyright © 2025 by Patricia Akinrogunde

All rights reserved. No portion of this book may be reproduced, stored in a retrieval system, or transmitted in any form or by any means – electronic, mechanical, photocopy, recording, scanning, or other – except for brief quotations in critical reviews or articles, without the prior written permission of the publisher.

Published and Printed in the United States by the Triple Joy Group

ISBN 979-8-9996856-2-9

This 90 Day Triple Joy Leadership Journal: Olive Joy Faith Based Edition Reflection Journal Belongs to:

_____

TABLE OF CONTENTS

Introduction 1

How to Use This Journal 3

Week 1: Called to Lead 4

Week 2: Leading with Wisdom 18

Week 3: Leading Through Challenges 32

Week 4: Servant Leadership 46

Week 5: Vision-Fueled Leadership 60

Week 6: Leading with Integrity 74

Week 7: Empowering Others 88

Week 8: Hearing God's Voice 102

Week 9: Faith Over Fear 116

Week 10: Stewarding Influence 130

Week 11: Persevering in Purpose 144

Week 12: Leading with Hope 158

Week 13: Finishing Faithfully 172

Closing Reflection 184

Prayer of Commission 186

Keep Growing with the Triple Joy Group &
Olive Joy Ministries 188

About the Author 190

INTRODUCTION

Welcome to the Triple Joy Leadership Journal:
Olive Joy Faith-Based Edition

This journal is your 90-day companion to grow in faith, reflect with intention, and lead with clarity and spiritual boldness. Whether you're a church leader, business professional of faith, or both, this space invites you to lead from the overflow of God's presence in your life.

Rooted in the heart of Olive Joy Ministries and built on biblical truths, this journal helps you align your leadership with God's purpose for you.

At Olive Joy Ministries, we believe faithful leadership stands on three biblical pillars:

1. **Purpose** – *Embracing your God-given calling.*
2. **Joy** – *Finding strength and delight in the Lord as you lead.*
3. **Growth** – *Becoming more Christlike in character, wisdom, and influence.*

Each week begins with an encouraging scripture and a weekly focus, followed by a biblical leadership principle, reflection prompts, and a Spirit-led action plan. This journal is not about perfection—it's about obedience, grace, and Spirit-empowered progress.

We are honored to walk alongside you as you lead with the joy of the Lord.

> "Our greatest fear should not be of failure, but of succeeding at something that doesn't really matter."
> — **D.L. Moody**

HOW TO USE THIS JOURNAL

Start each week with the scripture and weekly focus. Meditate and pray through it.

Reflect intentionally on the biblical leadership insight and journal your thoughts.

Act with purpose using the space provided for your action steps, daily gratitude, answered prayers, and leadership wins.

Wrap up the week by celebrating growth, documenting God's faithfulness, and preparing for the week ahead.

You don't need to have it all figured out.

You simply need a willing heart, a teachable spirit, and the courage to follow God's lead.

Let's begin—together, with faith and joy.

WEEK 1
Called to Lead

"The LORD will make you the head, not the tail. If you pay attention to the commands of the LORD your God that I give you this day and carefully follow them, you will always be at the top, never at the bottom."
— Deuteronomy 28:13 (NIV)

Recognizing your divine calling and stepping into it with confidence.

God doesn't call the qualified—He qualifies the called. As a leader of faith, your authority doesn't come from a title, platform, or position; it comes from obedience to God's call. Leadership in the Kingdom is about servanthood, stewardship, and walking by faith, not by sight.

When you understand that your leadership is rooted in God's choosing, it frees you from striving to prove yourself to others. The world often measures leaders by influence, charisma, or results, but in God's Kingdom, leadership is measured by faithfulness. To be "the head and not the tail" is not about personal pride but about walking in alignment with His Word so you can serve as a channel of His wisdom, peace, and direction.

Your calling is also a responsibility. God places you in leadership not for self-promotion, but for Kingdom impact. When you lead with integrity, courage, and humility, others are drawn to Christ through your example. As you step boldly into your role, remember: it is not your strength that sustains you, but His Spirit working in and through you.

REFLECTION QUESTIONS

1. How do you currently define your calling?

   _____
   _____
   _____
   _____

2. Where have you felt God nudging you to step up or step out in leadership?

   _____
   _____
   _____
   _____

3. What fears, doubts, or distractions have tried to hold you back?

   _____
   _____
   _____
   _____

4. In what ways do you sense God confirming your leadership assignment in this season?

   _____
   _____
   _____
   _____

WEEKLY ACTION PLAN

This week, I will take one step to walk confidently in my calling by:

_____
_____
_____
_____
_____
_____

A small change I can make to embrace my God-given identity as a leader:

_____
_____
_____
_____
_____
_____

Day 1 – Embracing the Call

Today's Date: _____

Morning Prayer / Scripture Meditation:

Reflect on Deuteronomy 28:13. What does being "the head and not the tail" mean to you?

_____
_____
_____

Leadership Intention:

Today, I will walk in confidence that God has called me. How?

_____
_____
_____

Key Action Step:

What step of obedience or courage will I take today?

_____
_____
_____

Gratitude Moment:

Today I thank God for...

_____
_____
_____

Leadership Win:

One victory or moment of growth I experienced today was...

_____
_____
_____

Day 2 – God Qualifies the Called

Today's Date: _____

Morning Prayer / Scripture Meditation:

Prayerfully consider how God equips you for leadership.

_____

_____

_____

Leadership Intention:

Today, I will depend on God's strength, not my own.

_____

_____

_____

Key Action Step:

One area where I will stop striving and trust God is…

_____

_____

_____

Gratitude Moment:

Today, I thank God for giving me the gift of…

_____

_____

_____

Leadership Win:

Today's victory or lesson was…

_____

_____

_____

Day 3 – Walking by Faith

Today's Date: _____

Morning Prayer / Scripture Meditation:

Ask God for courage to take a bold step today.

_____
_____
_____

Leadership Intention:

Today, I will choose faith over fear. How?

_____
_____
_____

Key Action Step:

One faith-filled action I will take is…

_____
_____
_____

Gratitude Moment:

Today, I thank God for His faithfulness when…

_____
_____
_____

Leadership Win:

Today's victory or growth was…

_____
_____
_____

Day 4 – Servanthood in Calling

Today's Date: _____

Morning Prayer / Scripture Meditation:

Meditate on Jesus' model of servant leadership.

_____

_____

_____

Leadership Intention:

Today, I will lead by serving others first.

_____

_____

_____

Key Action Step:

One act of service I will intentionally do today is…

_____

_____

_____

Gratitude Moment:

Today, I thank God for leaders who served me by…

_____

_____

_____

Leadership Win:

Today's victory or reflection was…

_____

_____

_____

Day 5 – Bold Obedience

Today's Date: _____

Morning Prayer / Scripture Meditation:

Declare your willingness to obey God fully.

_____
_____
_____

Leadership Intention:

Today, I will walk in bold obedience. How?

_____
_____
_____

Key Action Step:

One hard but necessary step of obedience I will take is…

_____
_____
_____

Gratitude Moment:

Today, I thank God for guiding me when…

_____
_____
_____

Leadership Win:

Today's victory or lesson was…

_____
_____
_____

Day 6 – Confidence in Christ

Today's Date: _____

Morning Prayer / Scripture Meditation:

Remember that your confidence comes from Christ, not comparison.

_____

_____

_____

Leadership Intention:

Today, I will lead with confidence rooted in Christ. How?

_____

_____

_____

Key Action Step:

One affirmation I will declare today is…

_____

_____

_____

Gratitude Moment:

Today, I thank God for the opportunity to…

_____

_____

_____

Leadership Win:

Today's victory or encouragement was…

_____

_____

_____

Day 7 – Rest & Reflection

Today's Date: _____

Morning Prayer / Scripture Meditation:

Thank God for His leadership over your life this week.

_____
_____
_____

Rest Intention

Today, I will rest in God's calling, not my striving.

_____
_____
_____

Reflection Highlight:

The most meaningful leadership lesson I learned this week is…

_____
_____
_____

Gratitude Moment:

Today, I thank God for three blessings from this week:

_____
_____
_____

Worship Note / Song / Scripture:

A word, song, or scripture that lifted me this week was…

_____
_____
_____

END-OF-WEEK WRAP-UP

What did God teach you this week about leadership?

_____
_____
_____
_____

How did you experience His presence, provision, or confirmation?

_____
_____
_____
_____

What's one thing you're celebrating?

_____
_____
_____
_____

What's one thing you're praying over for next week?

_____
_____
_____
_____

WEEK 2
Leading with Wisdom

"If any of you lacks wisdom, you should ask God, who gives generously to all without finding fault, and it will be given to you."
— James 1:5 (NIV)

Seeking and applying godly wisdom in every leadership decision.

Wise leadership begins with humility and dependence on God. While strategy and experience have their place, true insight comes from above. Leaders who seek God's wisdom create cultures of discernment, clarity, and peace. In a world where quick fixes and surface-level solutions are often celebrated, the leader who pauses to seek divine direction stands out as steady, discerning, and trustworthy. Wisdom is not only about what you know but also about how you apply knowledge with grace and integrity.

Godly wisdom helps you discern the difference between what is good and what is best. It teaches you to look beyond short-term gains and focus on long-term Kingdom impact. A wise leader doesn't simply react to problems but prayerfully responds with discernment, weighing every choice against God's Word and the values of His Kingdom. This kind of leadership fosters confidence among those you serve, because they see that your decisions are rooted in more than human reasoning — they are anchored in divine counsel.

Finally, wisdom protects leaders from pride and burnout. It reminds us that we don't have to carry the weight of every decision alone. By seeking God's wisdom daily, you acknowledge that His perspective is higher and His understanding greater than yours. This posture of reliance not only strengthens your leadership but also models to others the importance of humility, prayer, and trust in God's guidance. Wise leaders create ripple effects of peace, stability, and hope in their communities.

REFLECTION QUESTIONS

1. Where in your leadership do you most need God's wisdom right now?

2. How do you typically discern between your own understanding and God's guidance?

3. What habits or rhythms help you stay spiritually attuned as a leader?

4. Who in your life models wise, Spirit-led leadership?

WEEKLY ACTION PLAN

This week, I will take one step to seek God's wisdom in my leadership by:

_____
_____
_____
_____
_____
_____

A small change I can make to align my decisions more closely with God's Word:

_____
_____
_____
_____
_____
_____

Day 8 – Asking for Wisdom

Today's Date: _____

Morning Prayer / Scripture Meditation:
Prayerfully reflect on James 1:5. Where do you need God's wisdom today?

_____

_____

_____

Leadership Intention:
Today, I will seek God's wisdom before making decisions. How?

_____

_____

_____

Key Action Step:
One decision I will bring to God in prayer is…

_____

_____

_____

Gratitude Moment:
Today, I thank God for…

_____

_____

_____

Leadership Win:
Today's victory or growth was…

_____

_____

_____

Day 9 – Wisdom Over Strategy

Today's Date: _____

Morning Prayer / Scripture Meditation:

Invite God to give you insight that goes beyond human logic.

_____
_____
_____

Leadership Intention:

Today, I will prioritize God's perspective over my own plans. How?

_____
_____
_____

Key Action Step:

One area where I will shift from self-reliance to God-reliance is…

_____
_____
_____

Gratitude Moment:

Today, I thank God for a time He gave me clarity beyond my own understanding…

_____
_____
_____

Leadership Win:

Today's breakthrough or reflection was…

_____
_____
_____

Day 10 – Discerning What's Best

Today's Date: _____

Morning Prayer / Scripture Meditation:

Ask God for discernment between what is good and what is best.

_____
_____
_____

Leadership Intention:

Today, I will choose what aligns with God's heart, not just what looks good. How?

_____
_____
_____

Key Action Step:

One choice I will examine carefully today is…

_____
_____
_____

Gratitude & Growth:

Today, I thank God for guiding me through…

_____
_____
_____

Leadership Win:

Today's learning or growth moment was…

_____
_____
_____

Day 11 – Leading with Peace

Today's Date: _____

Morning Prayer / Scripture Meditation:

Prayerfully invite God's peace to guide your decisions today.

_____
_____
_____

Leadership Intention:

Today, I will lead in a way that cultivates peace and clarity. How?

_____
_____
_____

Key Action Step:

One way I will create peace for those I lead is…

_____
_____
_____

Gratitude & Growth:

Today, I thank God for His peace in…

_____
_____
_____

Leadership Win:

Today's encouraging moment was…

_____
_____
_____

Day 12 – Humility Brings Wisdom

Today's Date: _____

Morning Prayer / Scripture Meditation:

Reflect on how humility opens the door to wisdom.

_____

_____

_____

Leadership Intention:

Today, I will stay teachable and humble. How?

_____

_____

_____

Key Action Step:

One way I will seek feedback or wise counsel today is…

_____

_____

_____

Gratitude & Growth:

Today, I thank God for wise leaders who…

_____

_____

_____

Leadership Win:

Today's growth or confirmation was…

_____

_____

_____

Day 13 – Living the Word

Today's Date: _____

Morning Prayer / Scripture Meditation:

Read a passage of Scripture and ask: how can I apply this today?

_____

_____

_____

Leadership Intention:

Today, I will put God's Word into action. How?

_____

_____

_____

Key Action Step:

One verse I will live out practically today is…

_____

_____

_____

Gratitude & Growth:

Today, I thank God for His Word that…

_____

_____

_____

Leadership Win:

Today's evidence of growth was…

_____

_____

_____

Day 14 – Living the Word

Today's Date: _____

Morning Prayer / Scripture Meditation:

Thank God for generously providing wisdom when you ask.

_____
_____
_____

Rest Intention:

Today, I will rest in the assurance that God leads me wisely.

_____
_____
_____

Reflection Highlight:

The most important wisdom I gained this week is…

_____
_____
_____

Gratitude Moment:

Today, I thank God for three ways He gave me clarity this week:

_____
_____
_____

Worship Note / Song / Scripture:

A word, song, or scripture that carried me this week was…

_____
_____
_____

END-OF-WEEK WRAP-UP

What area of your leadership was most impacted by seeking God's wisdom?

_____
_____
_____
_____

What lesson or insight stood out the most?

_____
_____
_____
_____

What breakthrough or blessing came as a result of obedience this week?

_____
_____
_____
_____

What are you believing God for in the week ahead?

_____
_____
_____
_____

WEEK 3
Leading Through Challenges

"Have I not commanded you? Be strong and courageous. Do not be afraid; do not be discouraged, for the LORD your God will be with you wherever you go."
— Joshua 1:9 (NIV)

Embracing courage and God's presence in the face of leadership obstacles.

Challenges are not a sign of failure—they're opportunities for faith to rise. Every leader encounters opposition, setbacks, and seasons of pressure. The key is not in avoiding the storm, but in trusting the One who calms it. Just as Joshua faced the daunting task of leading God's people into the Promised Land, you too are called to lead with courage that flows from God's presence. The reminder "be strong and courageous" is not a suggestion; it is a command that acknowledges the reality of difficulty but anchors you in the certainty of God's faithfulness.

When obstacles come, it's easy to feel overwhelmed or disqualified. Yet, challenges are the very soil where resilience, perseverance, and deeper faith are cultivated. Leaders who endure hardship with unwavering trust in God not only grow personally but also inspire those around them. By choosing faith over fear, you demonstrate that leadership is not about having all the answers but about knowing the One who does. God's presence doesn't always remove the challenge, but it always equips you to face it with strength beyond your own.

True leadership in the Kingdom is revealed in how you respond under pressure. Challenges refine your character, test your motives, and purify your vision. When you remain steadfast in prayer and lean on God's promises, you become a steady example of courage and hope. Others will look to you, not because you avoided hardship, but because you faced it with unwavering faith in the God who never leaves nor forsakes His people.

REFLECTION QUESTIONS

1. What challenge are you currently facing in your leadership?

   _____
   _____
   _____
   _____

2. How do you typically respond under pressure?

   _____
   _____
   _____
   _____

3. What past victories remind you that God is faithful?

   _____
   _____
   _____
   _____

4. How can you model courage and resilience to those you lead?

   _____
   _____
   _____
   _____

WEEKLY ACTION PLAN

This week, I will take one step to face challenges with courage and faith by:

_____
_____
_____
_____
_____

A small change I can make to trust God more deeply in difficulties:

_____
_____
_____
_____
_____
_____

Day 15 – Courage Commanded

Today's Date: _____

Morning Prayer / Scripture Meditation:

Read Joshua 1:9. Where do you need to be reminded to be strong and courageous?

_____
_____
_____

Leadership Intention:

Today, I will choose courage over fear.

_____
_____
_____

Key Action Step:

One fear I will surrender to God today is...

_____
_____
_____

Gratitude & Growth:

Today, I thank God for being with me when...

_____
_____
_____

Leadership Win:

Today's moment of courage was...

_____
_____
_____

Day 16 – Faith in the Storm

Today's Date: _____

Morning Prayer / Scripture Meditation:

Invite God's peace into a current challenge you face.

_____

_____

_____

Leadership Intention:

Today, I will trust God in the middle of uncertainty.

_____

_____

_____

Key Action Step:

One storm I will choose to face with faith is…

_____

_____

_____

Gratitude & Growth:

Today, I thank God for calming my heart when…

_____

_____

_____

Leadership Win:

Today's growth in faith was…

_____

_____

_____

Day 17 – Growth Under Pressure

Today's Date: _____

Morning Prayer / Scripture Meditation:

Ask God to strengthen your character through challenges.

_____

_____

_____

Leadership Intention:

Today, I will see challenges as opportunities to grow.

_____

_____

_____

Key Action Step:

One lesson God is teaching me in this challenge is…

_____

_____

_____

Gratitude & Growth:

Today, I thank God for shaping me through…

_____

_____

_____

Leadership Win:

Today's evidence of resilience was…

_____

_____

_____

Day 18 – Resisting Discouragement

Today's Date: _____

Morning Prayer / Scripture Meditation:

Prayerfully ask God to guard your heart from discouragement.

Leadership Intention:

Today, I will not let discouragement control my decisions.

Key Action Step:

One negative thought I will replace with God's truth is…

Gratitude & Growth:

Today, I thank God for encouragement I received through…

Leadership Win:

Today's reflection or breakthrough was…

Day 19 – Example in Hardship

Today's Date: _____

Morning Prayer / Scripture Meditation:
Ask God to make your leadership an example of hope.

_____

_____

_____

Leadership Intention:
Today, I will lead by example, even in difficulty.

_____

_____

_____

Key Action Step:
One way I can model faith to others today is…

_____

_____

_____

Gratitude & Growth:
Today, I thank God for people watching my example who…

_____

_____

_____

Leadership Win:
Today's encouraging impact was…

_____

_____

_____

Day 20 – God's Presence Sustains

Today's Date: _____

Morning Prayer / Scripture Meditation:

Reflect on God's promise: "I will be with you wherever you go."

_____

_____

_____

Leadership Intention:

Today, I will rely on God's presence for strength.

_____

_____

_____

Key Action Step:

One way I will acknowledge God's presence today is…

_____

_____

Gratitude & Growth:

Today, I thank God for sustaining me through…

_____

_____

_____

Leadership Win:

Today's encouragement from His presence was…

_____

_____

_____

Day 21 – Rest & Reflection

Today's Date: _____

Morning Prayer / Scripture Meditation:

Thank God for walking with you through every challenge.

_____

_____

_____

Rest Intention:

Today, I will rest in God's strength, not my own.

_____

_____

_____

Reflection Highlight:

The greatest lesson I learned in challenges this week was…

_____

_____

_____

Gratitude Moment:

Today, I thank God for three ways He strengthened me this week:

_____

_____

_____

Worship Note / Song / Scripture:

A word, song, or scripture that gave me courage this week was…

_____

_____

_____

END-OF-WEEK WRAP-UP

What did you learn about yourself and God through this week's challenge?

_____
_____
_____
_____

How did you experience His strength or peace?

_____
_____
_____
_____

What breakthrough moment or encouragement stood out?

_____
_____
_____
_____

What are you carrying forward in faith next week?

_____
_____
_____
_____

WEEK 4
Servant Leadership

"Whoever wants to become great among you must be your servant, and whoever wants to be first must be your slave—just as the Son of Man did not come to be served, but to serve, and to give his life as a ransom for many."
— Matthew 20:26–28 (NIV)

Leading by example through humility, compassion, and service.

Jesus turned leadership on its head. In His Kingdom, greatness isn't measured by position or power but by how well we serve others. Servant leadership is not weakness—it is strength under control. When you choose to lead with humility and compassion, you reflect Christ's example of washing His disciples' feet. This model of leadership doesn't diminish your influence; it multiplies it, because people are drawn to leaders who genuinely care more about others than themselves.

Servant leadership demands a different posture—one that puts people before programs, souls before systems, and relationships before results. A servant leader listens with empathy, leads with integrity, and makes decisions not just for personal gain but for the well-being of those entrusted to their care. This way of leading nurtures trust, fosters unity, and creates an atmosphere where others feel valued and empowered. Far from being passive, servant leadership is an active choice to elevate others while faithfully stewarding the authority God has given you.

At its core, servant leadership is Christ-centered leadership. When you serve others, you model Jesus' heart to those who may never open a Bible but will read your life. True greatness in leadership is not found in recognition or applause but in quiet acts of sacrifice, encouragement, and consistency. As you lead by serving, you not only build stronger teams and communities but also honor God, who delights in leaders who reflect His Son's example.

REFLECTION QUESTIONS

1. How do you define servant leadership in your current context?

2. Where is God calling you to serve more selflessly?

3. Who in your life needs to see a Christ-like example of leadership?

4. What would change if you led more from love than from authority?

WEEKLY ACTION PLAN

This week, I will take one step to serve others with humility and compassion by:

_____
_____
_____
_____
_____
_____

A small change I can make to put people above position:

_____
_____
_____
_____
_____

Day 22 – Greatness Redefined

Today's Date: _____

Morning Prayer / Scripture Meditation:

Read Matthew 20:26-28. What does greatness look like in God's Kingdom compared to the world's view?

_____

_____

_____

Leadership Intention:

Today, I will lead by serving others first.

_____

_____

_____

Key Action Step:

One way I will put someone else's needs above my own today is…

_____

_____

_____

Gratitude Moment:

Today, I thank God for Jesus' model of servant leadership.

_____

_____

_____

Leadership Win:

Today's moment of humble service was…

_____

_____

_____

Day 23 – Strength Under Control

Today's Date: _____

Morning Prayer / Scripture Meditation:

Prayerfully ask God to help you use your influence with humility.

___

Leadership Intention:

Today, I will choose humility over pride.

___

Key Action Step:

One area where I will step back to let others shine is…

___

Gratitude Moment:

Today, I thank God for leaders who led with humility and impacted me by…

___

Leadership Win:

Today's reflection on humility was…

Day 24 – Compassion in Action

Today's Date: _____

Morning Prayer / Scripture Meditation:

Ask God to open your eyes to someone who needs encouragement today.

_____
_____
_____

Leadership Intention:

Today, I will lead with compassion.

_____
_____
_____

Key Action Step:

One intentional act of kindness I will show today is…

_____
_____
_____

Gratitude Moment:

Today, I thank God for moments when I was shown compassion.

_____
_____
_____

Leadership Win:

Today's impact through compassion was…

_____
_____
_____

Day 25 – Listening First

Today's Date: _____

Morning Prayer / Scripture Meditation:

Meditate on being quick to listen and slow to speak.

Leadership Intention:

Today, I will listen with empathy and patience.

Key Action Step:

One relationship I will strengthen by listening more is…

Gratitude Moment:

Today, I thank God for people who truly listened to me when…

Leadership Win:

Today's breakthrough in listening was…

Day 26 – Sacrifice and Service

Today's Date: _____

Morning Prayer / Scripture Meditation:

Reflect on how Jesus gave His life as a ransom for many.

_____

_____

_____

Leadership Intention:

Today, I will embrace sacrificial leadership.

_____

_____

_____

Key Action Step:

One small sacrifice I will make for someone else today is…

_____

_____

_____

Gratitude Moment:

Today, I thank God for the ultimate sacrifice of Christ.

_____

_____

_____

Leadership Win:

Today's growth in sacrificial service was…

_____

_____

_____

Day 27 – Servant-Hearted Leadership

Today's Date: _____

Morning Prayer / Scripture Meditation:

Prayerfully invite God to form a servant's heart in you.

_____

_____

_____

Leadership Intention:

Today, I will put people above tasks.

_____

_____

_____

Key Action Step:

One way I will intentionally encourage or invest in someone today is…

_____

_____

_____

Gratitude Moment:

Today, I thank God for entrusting me with people to serve.

_____

_____

_____

Leadership Win:

Today's moment of servant leadership was…

_____

_____

_____

Day 28 – Rest & Reflection

Today's Date: _____

Morning Prayer / Scripture Meditation:

Thank God for the opportunities He gave you to serve this week.

_____

_____

_____

Rest Intention:

Today, I will rest in the truth that true greatness is found in serving.

_____

_____

_____

Reflection Highlight:

The most meaningful moment of service I experienced this week was…

_____

_____

_____

Gratitude Moment:

Today, I thank God for three ways I saw humility expressed this week:

_____

_____

_____

Worship Note / Song / Scripture:

A word, song, or scripture that reminded me to serve this week was…

_____

_____

_____

END-OF-WEEK WRAP-UP

What did servant leadership look like in your life this week?

_____
_____
_____
_____

Who were you able to bless or encourage?

_____
_____
_____
_____

How did God refine your heart for leadership?

_____
_____
_____
_____

What insight or moment are you carrying into next week?

_____
_____
_____
_____

WEEK 5
Vision-Fueled Leadership

"Write the vision and make it plain on tablets, that he may run who reads it."
— Habakkuk 2:2 (NKJV)

Clarifying and communicating the God-given vision that fuels your leadership.

Vision gives purpose to your steps, clarity to your decisions, and endurance in hard seasons. Without vision, leadership becomes reactionary, tossed about by the demands of the moment. But when you have a clear, God-given vision, it becomes the compass that directs your path. A leader guided by divine vision sees beyond immediate challenges to the bigger picture of what God is building, which inspires confidence in those who follow.

Vision isn't just about big goals. It's about aligning with God's heart for your leadership. Many leaders chase after personal ambition, but Kingdom vision is birthed in prayer, obedience, and sensitivity to the Spirit's leading. It reflects not just where you want to go but where God is calling you to go. When you write the vision clearly and communicate it consistently, it brings focus to your team, helps align efforts, and keeps everyone pressing forward with shared purpose.

A God-given vision also provides endurance in hard seasons. When trials come and progress feels slow, vision reminds you why you began and who you are ultimately serving. It gives you the courage to keep moving forward when quitting feels easier. Vision is more than strategy—it is fuel for perseverance, a reminder that what you are building is not just for now, but for eternal impact. Leaders who cling to God's vision not only run with purpose themselves but also empower others to run with them in unity and faith.

REFLECTION QUESTIONS

1. What vision has God placed in your heart for this season?

   _____
   _____
   _____
   _____

2. Is your current pace, plan, or team aligned with that vision?

   _____
   _____
   _____
   _____

3. What distractions or doubts do you need to surrender?

   _____
   _____
   _____

4. Who can help you carry and communicate this vision?

   _____
   _____
   _____
   _____

WEEKLY ACTION PLAN

This week, I will take one step to clarify and communicate God's vision for my leadership by:

_____
_____
_____
_____
_____
_____

A small change I can make to align my actions more closely with His vision:

_____
_____
_____
_____
_____

Day 29 – Writing the Vision

Today's Date: _____

Morning Prayer / Scripture Meditation:

Read Habakkuk 2:2. What vision has God placed in your heart?

_____

_____

_____

Leadership Intention:

Today, I will clarify the vision God has given me.

_____

_____

_____

Key Action Step:

One sentence that captures God's vision for me is…

_____

_____

_____

Gratitude Moment:

Today, I thank God for entrusting me with vision.

_____

_____

_____

Leadership Win:

Today's breakthrough in clarity was…

_____

_____

_____

Day 30 – Vision Brings Focus

Today's Date: _____

Morning Prayer / Scripture Meditation:

Ask God to remove distractions and sharpen your focus.

_____

_____

_____

Leadership Intention:

Today, I will align my actions with God's vision.

_____

_____

_____

Key Action Step:

One distraction I will let go of to pursue vision is…

_____

_____

_____

Gratitude Moment:

Today, I thank God for clarity He gave me when…

_____

_____

_____

Leadership Win:

Today's focused step was…

_____

_____

_____

Day 31 – Sharing the Vision

Today's Date: _____

Morning Prayer / Scripture Meditation:
Prayerfully ask God for boldness to communicate vision clearly.

_____
_____
_____

Leadership Intention:
Today, I will share God's vision with confidence.

_____
_____
_____

Key Action Step:
One person I will share my vision with this week is…

_____
_____
_____

Gratitude Moment:
Today, I thank God for those who support His vision in me.

_____
_____
_____

Leadership Win:
Today's confirmation through others was…

_____
_____
_____

Day 32 – Running with Vision

Today's Date: _____

Morning Prayer / Scripture Meditation:

Ask God for strength to take action toward His vision.

_____

_____

_____

Leadership Intention:

Today, I will take steps toward God's vision.

_____

_____

_____

Key Action Step:

One practical step I can take toward my vision today is…

_____

_____

_____

Gratitude Moment:

Today, I thank God for endurance on the journey.

_____

_____

_____

Leadership Win:

Today's progress in action was…

_____

_____

_____

Day 33 – Endurance in Vision

Today's Date: _____

Morning Prayer / Scripture Meditation:

Meditate on perseverance in pursuing vision.

_____

_____

_____

Leadership Intention:

Today, I will remain steadfast in God's vision.

_____

_____

_____

Key Action Step:

One way I will persevere in vision despite challenges is…

_____

_____

_____

Gratitude Moment:

Today, I thank God for His perfect timing.

_____

_____

_____

Leadership Win:

Today's endurance in vision was…

_____

_____

_____

Day 34 – Aligning with God's Heart

Today's Date: _____

Morning Prayer / Scripture Meditation:

Prayerfully ask God to align your vision with His Kingdom purpose.

_____
_____
_____

Leadership Intention:

Today, I will ensure my vision glorifies God.

_____
_____
_____

Key Action Step:

One way my vision will serve others is…

_____
_____
_____

Gratitude Moment:

Today, I thank God for shaping my vision to reflect His heart.

_____
_____
_____

Leadership Win:

Today's confirmation of alignment was…

_____
_____
_____

Day 35 – Rest & Reflection

Today's Date: _____

Morning Prayer / Scripture Meditation:
Thank God for the vision He has entrusted to you.

_____

_____

_____

Rest Intention:
Today, I will rest knowing the vision belongs to God.

_____

_____

_____

Reflection Highlight:
The clearest part of God's vision I discovered this week was…

_____

_____

_____

Gratitude Moment:
Today, I thank God for three ways He confirmed vision this week:

_____

_____

_____

Worship Note / Song / Scripture:
A word, song, or scripture that strengthened my vision this week was…

_____

_____

_____

END-OF-WEEK WRAP-UP

How has your vision become clearer this week?

_____

_____

_____

_____

What actions did you take to align with and communicate that vision?

_____

_____

_____

_____

Where did you see confirmation or new direction from God?

_____

_____

_____

_____

What will you do next week to walk out that vision more fully?

_____

_____

_____

_____

WEEK 6
Leading with Integrity

"The integrity of the upright guides them, but the unfaithful are destroyed by their duplicity."
— Proverbs 11:3 (NIV)

Choosing honesty, consistency, and character in every leadership decision.

Integrity is the invisible foundation of lasting leadership. It's who you are when no one is watching. Your influence deepens when your words and actions match. A leader without integrity may impress people for a moment, but a leader with integrity impacts people for a lifetime. When those around you see that your character is consistent in both public and private, their trust in your leadership grows stronger, and your example points them back to Christ.

Integrity means choosing the harder right over the easier wrong. It requires honesty when a lie might seem more convenient and faithfulness when compromise could appear beneficial. Leaders who walk in integrity don't shift with circumstances or bend under pressure—they remain steady, guided by God's truth. This kind of character not only protects your reputation but also safeguards your heart, ensuring your leadership remains anchored in righteousness rather than swayed by pride or personal gain.

Integrity also multiplies influence. When people know they can count on your word, they follow with confidence. Trust becomes the glue that holds teams, communities, and ministries together, and it begins with leaders who refuse to compromise their values. Ultimately, leading with integrity honors God, who sees every hidden choice. Your commitment to integrity reminds others that true success in leadership isn't measured by titles or achievements but by faithfulness to God and His principles.

REFLECTION QUESTIONS

1. Where do I feel most challenged to lead with greater integrity?

   _____
   _____
   _____
   _____

2. Are there any habits or decisions that I need to surrender or realign?

   _____
   _____
   _____
   _____

3. How does my leadership reflect the character of Christ?

   _____
   _____
   _____
   _____

4. Who looks to me as an example of consistent, Godly leadership?

   _____
   _____
   _____
   _____

WEEKLY ACTION PLAN

This week, I will take one step to live consistently with my values by:

_____
_____
_____
_____
_____
_____

A small change I can make to strengthen my integrity in leadership:

_____
_____
_____
_____
_____
_____

Day 36 – Integrity Guides You

Today's Date: _____

Morning Prayer / Scripture Meditation:

Read Proverbs 11:3. How does integrity serve as your compass?

_____

_____

_____

Leadership Intention:

Today, I will let integrity guide my choices.

_____

_____

_____

Key Action Step:

One decision I will make with honesty today is…

_____

_____

_____

Gratitude Moment:

Today, I thank God for being a God of truth.

_____

_____

_____

Leadership Win:

Today's moment of walking in integrity was…

_____

_____

_____

Day 37 – Who You Are in Secret

Today's Date: _____

Morning Prayer / Scripture Meditation:

Ask God to shape your character in private as much as in public.

_____
_____
_____

Leadership Intention:

Today, I will be consistent in every area of my life.

_____
_____
_____

Key Action Step:

One hidden area where I will practice greater integrity is…

_____
_____
_____

Gratitude Moment:

Today, I thank God for His mercy and grace in my weaknesses.

_____
_____
_____

Leadership Win:

Today's growth in private character was…

_____
_____
_____

Day 38 – Choosing the Hard Right

Today's Date: _____

Morning Prayer / Scripture Meditation:
Prayerfully ask God for courage to choose the harder right over the easier wrong.

_____

_____

_____

Leadership Intention:
Today, I will not compromise for convenience.

_____

_____

_____

Key Action Step:
One situation where I will choose the hard right is…

_____

_____

_____

Gratitude Moment:
Today, I thank God for the Spirit who strengthens me to choose wisely.

_____

_____

_____

Leadership Win:
Today's courageous decision was…

_____

_____

_____

Day 39 – Consistency Builds Trust

Today's Date: _____

Morning Prayer / Scripture Meditation:

Reflect on how consistency creates credibility in leadership.

_____
_____
_____

Leadership Intention:

Today, I will be dependable and consistent.

_____
_____
_____

Key Action Step:

One way I will demonstrate consistency today is…

_____
_____
_____

Gratitude Moment:

Today, I thank God for trustworthy people in my life.

_____
_____
_____

Leadership Win:

Today's example of consistency was…

_____
_____
_____

Day 40 – Honoring God in Integrity

Today's Date: _____

Morning Prayer / Scripture Meditation:

Consider how your choices today can honor God.

_____
_____
_____

Leadership Intention:

Today, I will honor God with my decisions.

_____
_____
_____

Key Action Step:

One choice I will make today that glorifies God is...

_____
_____
_____

Gratitude Moment:

Today, I thank God for His unchanging faithfulness.

_____
_____
_____

Leadership Win:

Today's honoring decision was...

_____
_____
_____

Day 41 – Integrity Multiplies Influence

Today's Date: _____

Morning Prayer / Scripture Meditation:

Ask God to expand your influence through your character.

_____

_____

_____

Leadership Intention:

Today, I will inspire trust by living with integrity.

_____

_____

_____

Key Action Step:

One way my integrity can encourage someone else today is…

_____

_____

_____

Gratitude Moment:

Today, I thank God for the influence He entrusts to me.

_____

_____

_____

Leadership Win:

Today's influence through integrity was…

_____

_____

_____

Day 42 – Rest & Reflection

Today's Date: _____

Morning Prayer / Scripture Meditation:

Thank God for being your constant guide in truth.

_____

_____

_____

Rest Intention:

Today, I will rest in the peace of a clean conscience.

_____

_____

_____

Reflection Highlight:

One moment where integrity guided me most this week was…

_____

_____

_____

Gratitude Moment:

Today, I thank God for three ways He helped me stay consistent this week:

_____

_____

_____

Worship Note / Song / Scripture:

A word, song, or scripture that reminded me to live with integrity this week was…

_____

_____

_____

END-OF-WEEK WRAP-UP

Where did integrity guide your leadership this week?

___

What tested your values—and how did you respond?

___

How did God affirm or stretch your character?

___

What commitments are you making moving forward?

___

WEEK 7
Empowering Others

> "And let us consider how we may spur one another on toward love and good deeds."
> — Hebrews 10:24 (NIV)

Multiplying impact by equipping, encouraging, and elevating others.

Great leaders activate others. When you empower others, you create space for growth, creativity, and legacy. Leadership isn't about keeping influence to yourself—it's about multiplying it by raising up others to walk in their God-given callings. Empowering others requires intentional encouragement, trust, and a willingness to release control. Just as Jesus sent out His disciples with authority, we too are called to equip and release those around us to lead and serve.

When you empower others, you communicate value. You tell people, "I see you, I believe in you, and I know God can use you." This lifts hearts, sparks creativity, and stirs courage. People thrive when they know their gifts are recognized and their contributions matter. Empowering leadership is not about competition but about collaboration—it's about building a culture where everyone flourishes because everyone's role is honored.

Empowering others also extends your legacy. Long after your season of leadership shifts, the people you've invested in will continue to carry forward the vision and values you modeled. Leadership that hoards power dies with the leader, but leadership that equips others lives on for generations. When you intentionally develop and release others, you reflect the heart of Christ, who poured into His followers so that they could carry the Gospel to the ends of the earth.

REFLECTION QUESTIONS

1. Who in your circle or team needs to be empowered right now?

2. Are you delegating with trust or micromanaging from fear?

3. How are you intentionally developing leaders around you?

4. What does "leadership multiplication" look like in your context?

WEEKLY ACTION PLAN

This week, I will take one step to equip or encourage someone I lead by:

_____
_____
_____
_____
_____
_____

A small change I can make to release more responsibility and trust others:

_____
_____
_____
_____
_____
_____

Day 43 – Activating Potential

Today's Date: _____

Morning Prayer / Scripture Meditation:

Read Hebrews 10:24. Who around you needs encouragement to step into their God-given potential?

Leadership Intention:

Today, I will call out the gifts in others.

Key Action Step:

One person I will encourage to grow today is…

Gratitude Moment:

Today, I thank God for those who saw potential in me when…

Leadership Win:

Today's moment of activating someone's potential was…

Day 44 – Creating Space to Grow

Today's Date: _____

Morning Prayer / Scripture Meditation:

Prayerfully ask God to help you release control and allow others to rise.

_____
_____
_____

Leadership Intention:

Today, I will give space for others to lead and grow.

_____
_____
_____

Key Action Step:

One responsibility I can delegate or share is…

_____
_____
_____

Gratitude Moment:

Today, I thank God for leaders who trusted me with responsibility.

_____
_____
_____

Leadership Win:

Today's empowering action was…

_____
_____
_____

Day 45 – Speaking Life

Today's Date: _____

Morning Prayer / Scripture Meditation:

Ask God to give you words that build up and not tear down.

_____
_____
_____

Leadership Intention:

Today, I will use my words to strengthen others.

_____
_____
_____

Key Action Step:

One affirmation or encouragement I will share today is…

_____
_____
_____

Gratitude Moment:

Today, I thank God for the power of life-giving words.

_____
_____
_____

Leadership Win:

Today's impact through encouragement was…

_____
_____
_____

Day 46 – Investing in Others

Today's Date: _____

Morning Prayer / Scripture Meditation:

Prayerfully ask God who you should invest in this season.

_____

_____

_____

Leadership Intention:

Today, I will pour into the growth of others.

_____

_____

_____

Key Action Step:

One way I will mentor, teach, or equip someone today is…

_____

_____

Gratitude Moment:

Today, I thank God for mentors who invested in me.

_____

_____

_____

Leadership Win:

Today's investment moment was…

_____

_____

_____

Day 47 – Legacy Through Others

Today's Date: _____

Morning Prayer / Scripture Meditation:

Reflect on how empowering others creates a lasting impact.

_____
_____
_____

Leadership Intention:

Today, I will lead with a legacy mindset.

_____
_____
_____

Key Action Step:

One way I will multiply my influence through others is…

_____
_____
_____

Gratitude Moment:

Today, I thank God for the opportunity to build beyond myself.

_____
_____
_____

Leadership Win:

Today's step toward legacy was…

_____
_____
_____

Day 48 – Trusting Others with Responsibility

Today's Date: _____

Morning Prayer / Scripture Meditation:

Ask God to strengthen your trust in those you lead.

_____
_____
_____

Leadership Intention:

Today, I will entrust responsibility so others can grow.

_____
_____
_____

Key Action Step:

One responsibility I will release to someone this week is…

_____
_____
_____

Gratitude Moment:

Today, I thank God for gifting my team/community with unique abilities.

_____
_____
_____

Leadership Win:

Today's evidence of trust was…

_____
_____
_____

Day 49 – Rest & Reflection

Today's Date: _____

Morning Prayer / Scripture Meditation:

Thank God for the people He has placed in your care.

_____

_____

_____

Rest Intention:

Today, I will rest knowing leadership is not about me, but about multiplication.

_____

_____

_____

Reflection Highlight:

The most meaningful way I empowered someone this week was…

_____

_____

_____

Gratitude Moment:

Today, I thank God for three ways He showed me the value of empowering others this week:

_____

_____

_____

Worship Note / Song / Scripture:

A word, song, or scripture that reminded me to invest in others this week was…

_____

_____

_____

END-OF-WEEK WRAP-UP

Who did you empower this week and how?

_____
_____
_____
_____

What did you learn about trust and leadership multiplication?

_____
_____
_____
_____

Where did you see fruit in letting go and building others up?

_____
_____
_____
_____

What next step can you take to keep growing as an empowering leader?

_____
_____
_____
_____

WEEK 8
Hearing God's Voice

"My sheep listen to my voice; I know them, and they follow me."
— John 10:27 (NIV)

Tuning your heart to hear God's direction in your leadership journey.

The most powerful leadership decisions come from internal stillness with God. The ability to hear God's voice is a sacred and vital part of faith-driven leadership. In a world filled with noise, distractions, and competing opinions, leaders who intentionally quiet their hearts before the Lord are able to discern His direction with clarity. It is not always in the earthquake, wind, or fire that God speaks, but often in the gentle whisper that requires humility, attentiveness, and faith.

Hearing God's voice reminds us that leadership is not about relying solely on human wisdom or strategy but about being guided by the Shepherd Himself. When you make space for prayer, worship, and time in His Word, you train your spirit to recognize His leading. As you follow His promptings, you'll often find doors opening, solutions appearing, and strength rising in ways that far surpass what human effort could accomplish. This dependence on God sets apart Kingdom leaders from those who lead in their own strength.

Obedience to God's voice is what transforms hearing into impact. It's one thing to listen, but another to act on what He says—even when it's uncomfortable or requires risk. Leaders who obey God's direction not only walk in greater confidence but also model to those they lead what it means to fully trust Him. By cultivating a life where God's voice is welcomed, prioritized, and obeyed, you ensure your leadership is aligned with His perfect will, bearing fruit that lasts for eternity.

REFLECTION QUESTIONS

1. What does "hearing God's voice" look like in your daily life?

   _____
   _____
   _____
   _____

2. What distractions might be clouding your spiritual hearing?

   _____
   _____
   _____
   _____

3. How do you test and confirm what you believe God is saying?

   _____
   _____
   _____
   _____

4. What recent decision or season needs divine direction?

   _____
   _____
   _____
   _____

WEEKLY ACTION PLAN

This week, I will take one step to quiet distractions and listen to God's voice by:

_____
_____
_____
_____
_____
_____

A small change I can make to respond more quickly to His direction:

_____
_____
_____
_____
_____
_____

Day 50 – The Shepherd's Voice

Today's Date: _____

Morning Prayer / Scripture Meditation:

Read John 10:27. What does it mean to you that Jesus knows you by name?

_____
_____
_____

Leadership Intention:

Today, I will listen closely for God's voice.

_____
_____
_____

Key Action Step:

One way I will pause to hear Him today is...

_____
_____
_____

Gratitude Moment:

Today, I thank God for speaking personally to me when...

_____
_____
_____

Leadership Win:

Today's moment of recognizing His voice was...

_____
_____
_____

Day 51 – Quieting the Noise

Today's Date: _____

Morning Prayer / Scripture Meditation:
Prayerfully ask God to quiet distractions so you can hear Him clearly.

Leadership Intention:
Today, I will seek stillness in His presence.

Key Action Step:
One distraction I will silence to hear God more clearly is…

Gratitude Moment:
Today, I thank God for His presence even in noisy places.

Leadership Win:
Today's step toward clarity was…

Day 52 – Scripture as Guidance

Today's Date: _____

Morning Prayer / Scripture Meditation:

Read a passage of Scripture and ask: "Lord, what are You saying to me today?"

_____

_____

_____

Leadership Intention:

Today, I will let God's Word guide my leadership.

_____

_____

_____

Key Action Step:

One decision I will align with Scripture today is…

_____

_____

_____

Gratitude Moment:

Today, I thank God for the gift of His Word.

_____

_____

_____

Leadership Win:

Today's evidence of God's direction was…

_____

_____

_____

Day 53 – Obedience to His Voice

Today's Date: _____

Morning Prayer / Scripture Meditation:

Prayerfully ask God for courage to obey what He says.

Leadership Intention:

Today, I will act on what God reveals.

Key Action Step:

One step of obedience I will take today is…

Gratitude Moment:

Today, I thank God for guiding me even when it stretched me.

Leadership Win:

Today's step of obedience was…

Day 54 – Testing the Voice

Today's Date: _____

Morning Prayer / Scripture Meditation:

Reflect on how God's voice is always consistent with His Word.

Leadership Intention:

Today, I will test what I hear against Scripture.

Key Action Step:

One impression or thought I will bring to Scripture for confirmation is…

Gratitude Moment:

Today, I thank God for discernment through His Spirit.

Leadership Win:

Today's confirmation of His voice was…

Day 55 – Hearing God in Community

Today's Date: _____

Morning Prayer / Scripture Meditation:

Prayerfully thank God for speaking through wise counsel.

_____
_____
_____

Leadership Intention:

Today, I will remain open to God's voice through others.

_____
_____
_____

Key Action Step:

One trusted person I will seek counsel from this week is…

_____
_____
_____

Gratitude Moment:

Today, I thank God for godly voices that encourage me.

_____
_____
_____

Leadership Win:

Today's affirmation through community was…

_____
_____
_____

Day 56 – Rest & Reflection

Today's Date: _____

Morning Prayer / Scripture Meditation:

Thank God for being your faithful Shepherd and guide.

_____

_____

_____

Rest Intention:

Today, I will rest in confidence that God still speaks.

_____

_____

_____

Reflection Highlight:

One key way I heard God's voice this week was…

_____

_____

_____

Gratitude Moment:

Today, I thank God for three ways He directed me this week:

_____

_____

_____

Worship Note / Song / Scripture:

A word, song, or scripture that reminded me of His voice this week was…

_____

_____

_____

END-OF-WEEK WRAP-UP

What did you hear God say to you this week?

___

How did that guidance impact your leadership?

___

Where did you experience confirmation or clarity?

___

How will you continue to cultivate a listening life?

___

WEEK 9
Faith Over Fear

"For God has not given us a spirit of fear, but of power and of love and of a sound mind.".
— 2 Timothy 1:7 (NKJV)

Choosing courage and faith in leadership, even when uncertainty surrounds you.

Fear paralyzes purpose. But faith—rooted in the character and promises of God—disarms fear and fuels bold obedience. Fear whispers "you can't," while faith declares "God can." Every leader faces moments where uncertainty looms large, and the temptation is to shrink back or play it safe. But leaders who trust God's Word learn that faith is not about denying challenges—it's about believing that God is bigger than the challenges.

Faith empowers leaders to take steps that may seem risky to others but are rooted in obedience to God's call. It gives you the courage to move forward when the path isn't fully clear and the strength to keep going when resistance comes. Fear keeps you stuck, but faith moves you forward. When your leadership is grounded in faith, you model to others that courage is not the absence of fear—it's choosing to believe God's promises in the face of it.

Walking in faith as a leader creates ripple effects of hope and confidence in those around you. Teams, families, and communities are strengthened when they see leaders anchored in God's truth rather than swayed by fear. Faith produces bold obedience—the kind that steps into new territory, launches God-given visions, and perseveres when the odds look impossible. Leaders who choose faith over fear become living testimonies of God's power, love, and faithfulness.

REFLECTION QUESTIONS

1. What fear has tried to silence your leadership voice?

2. How have you seen faith overcome fear in the past?

3. Where do you need to step out boldly this week?

4. What truth from God's Word can you declare over your situation?

WEEKLY ACTION PLAN

This week, I will take one step of bold faith despite fear by:
_____
_____
_____
_____
_____
_____

A small change I can make to strengthen my faith over my feelings:
_____
_____
_____
_____
_____
_____

Day 57 – Fear is Not From God

Today's Date: _____

Morning Prayer / Scripture Meditation:

Read 2 Timothy 1:7. Where do you need to reject fear today?

_____

_____

_____

Leadership Intention:

Today, I will recognize fear is not from God.

_____

_____

_____

Key Action Step:

One fear I will surrender in prayer today is…

_____

_____

_____

Gratitude Moment:

Today, I thank God for replacing fear with His peace when…

_____

_____

_____

Leadership Win:

Today's victory over fear was…

_____

_____

_____

Day 58 – Power in the Spirit

Today's Date: _____

Morning Prayer / Scripture Meditation:

Prayerfully ask God to strengthen you with His Spirit.

_____
_____
_____

Leadership Intention:

Today, I will lead with the Spirit's power, not my own.

_____
_____
_____

Key Action Step:

One area where I need to walk in spiritual authority today is…

_____
_____
_____

Gratitude Moment:

Today, I thank God for His power that carried me when…

_____
_____
_____

Leadership Win:

Today's evidence of Spirit-empowered leadership was…

_____
_____
_____

Day 59 – Leading in Love

Today's Date: _____

Morning Prayer / Scripture Meditation:

Meditate on God's love as the foundation of your leadership.

_____
_____
_____

Leadership Intention:

Today, I will let love drive out fear in my leadership.

_____
_____
_____

Key Action Step:

One act of love I will extend to someone today is…

_____
_____
_____

Gratitude Moment:

Today, I thank God for His perfect love that casts out fear.

_____
_____
_____

Leadership Win:

Today's breakthrough in leading with love was…

_____
_____
_____

Day 60 – A Sound Mind

Today's Date: _____

Morning Prayer / Scripture Meditation:

Ask God to renew your thoughts and bring clarity.

_____

_____

_____

Leadership Intention:

Today, I will walk in self-discipline and clarity of thought.

_____

_____

_____

Key Action Step:

One anxious thought I will replace with God's truth is…

_____

_____

_____

Gratitude Moment:

Today, I thank God for guarding my mind with His peace.

_____

_____

_____

Leadership Win:

Today's renewed mindset was…

_____

_____

_____

Day 61 – Boldness in Action

Today's Date: _____

Morning Prayer / Scripture Meditation:

Invite God to give you boldness in a leadership decision.

_____
_____
_____

Leadership Intention:

Today, I will take bold steps of faith.

_____
_____
_____

Key Action Step:

One action I will take today despite fear is…

_____
_____
_____

Gratitude Moment:

Today, I thank God for courage to act when…

_____
_____
_____

Leadership Win:

Today's step of boldness was…

_____
_____
_____

Day 62 – Faith Over Feelings

Today's Date: _____

Morning Prayer / Scripture Meditation:

Reflect on walking by faith and not by sight.

_____

_____

_____

Leadership Intention:

Today, I will choose faith over my feelings.

_____

_____

_____

Key Action Step:

One area where I will trust God's promise over my emotions is…

_____

_____

_____

Gratitude Moment:

Today, I thank God for His promises that anchor me.

_____

_____

_____

Leadership Win:

Today's faith-filled choice was…

_____

_____

_____

Day 63 – Rest & Reflection

Today's Date: _____

Morning Prayer / Scripture Meditation:

Thank God for giving you a spirit of power, love, and a sound mind.

_____

_____

_____

Rest Intention:

Today, I will rest in courage, knowing fear has no hold on me.

_____

_____

_____

Reflection Highlight:

The biggest area where I overcame fear with faith this week was…

_____

_____

_____

Gratitude Moment:

Today, I thank God for three victories of faith this week:

_____

_____

_____

Worship Note / Song / Scripture:

A word, song, or scripture that strengthened my faith this week was…

_____

_____

_____

END-OF-WEEK WRAP-UP

What step of faith did you take this week?

___

How did you see fear lose its grip?

___

What did God show you about His power and presence?

___

Where will you boldly go from here?

___

WEEK 10
Stewarding Influence

"So if you have not been trustworthy in handling worldly wealth, who will trust you with true riches?"
— Luke 16:11 (NIV)

Understanding and managing your God-given influence with humility and purpose.

Leadership is stewardship. Whether you're leading a ministry, a business, or a family, your leadership is a platform to reflect God's heart and multiply Kingdom impact. Influence is not something we own—it's something God entrusts to us for a season, and how we steward it determines the fruit it produces. A leader who treats influence as a gift approaches it with gratitude, humility, and responsibility, knowing that every decision carries weight in the lives of others.

Stewarding influence requires intentional alignment with God's values. Influence can be easily misused when it becomes about personal recognition, control, or gain. But Kingdom leaders understand that influence is not about elevating themselves—it's about elevating Christ and serving people. When your decisions flow from prayer, integrity, and obedience, your influence creates life-giving impact, pointing others back to God as the true source of wisdom and authority.

When you steward influence well, you inspire and empower others to steward theirs. Healthy leadership multiplies because it equips people to carry vision, make wise choices, and live with integrity in their own spheres of influence. Influence isn't just about what you accomplish during your time of leadership—it's about the legacy you leave behind. Leaders who steward influence with humility and purpose leave behind a trail of transformed lives, strengthened communities, and Kingdom impact that outlives them.

REFLECTION QUESTIONS

1. What areas of influence has God entrusted to you right now?

2. Are there any places where your stewardship could be more intentional?

3. How can you use your platform to build others and glorify God?

4. What legacy do you want your leadership to leave?

WEEKLY ACTION PLAN

This week, I will take one step to use my influence to glorify God and serve others by:

_____
_____
_____
_____
_____
_____

A small change I can make to guard my influence with humility:

_____
_____
_____
_____
_____
_____

HOLY BIBLE

Day 64 – Influence as Stewardship

Today's Date: _____

Morning Prayer / Scripture Meditation:

Read Luke 16:11. What does it mean to view influence as something entrusted to you?

_____
_____
_____

Leadership Intention:

Today, I will treat my influence as a gift to steward, not a possession to keep.

_____
_____
_____

Key Action Step:

One area of influence I will handle more responsibly today is…

_____
_____
_____

Gratitude Moment:

Today, I thank God for entrusting me with…

_____
_____
_____

Leadership Win:

Today's example of stewarding influence was…

_____
_____
_____

Day 65 – Influence with Integrity

Today's Date: _____

Morning Prayer / Scripture Meditation:
Prayerfully ask God to help you manage influence with honesty.

Leadership Intention:
Today, I will align my influence with integrity.

Key Action Step:
One way I will be transparent in leadership today is…

Gratitude Moment:
Today, I thank God for trustworthy leaders who inspired me.

Leadership Win:
Today's moment of integrity in influence was…

Day 66 – Influence that Elevates Others

Today's Date: _____

Morning Prayer / Scripture Meditation:

Ask God to show you how to use your influence to uplift others.

Leadership Intention:

Today, I will use my influence to build others up, not myself.

Key Action Step:

One person I can intentionally encourage with my influence today is…

Gratitude Moment:

Today, I thank God for those who used their influence to bless me.

Leadership Win:

Today's encouragement through influence was…

Day 67 – Guarding Your Influence

Today's Date: _____

Morning Prayer / Scripture Meditation:

Prayerfully ask God to protect your testimony and reputation.

Leadership Intention:

Today, I will guard my influence by making wise choices.

Key Action Step:

One boundary I will set to protect my influence is…

Gratitude Moment:

Today, I thank God for guiding my steps away from temptation.

Leadership Win:

Today's protected moment of integrity was…

Day 68 – Influence with Eternal Impact

Today's Date: _____

Morning Prayer / Scripture Meditation:

Reflect on how your influence can have eternal consequences.

_____

_____

_____

Leadership Intention:

Today, I will live for eternal fruit, not temporary applause.

_____

_____

_____

Key Action Step:

One way I will point others to Christ with my influence today is…

_____

_____

_____

Gratitude Moment:

Today, I thank God for opportunities to impact eternity.

_____

_____

_____

Leadership Win:

Today's eternal influence moment was…

_____

_____

_____

Day 69 – Humility in Influence

Today's Date: _____

Morning Prayer / Scripture Meditation:

Ask God to keep you humble as He expands your influence.

_____
_____
_____

Leadership Intention:

Today, I will remember that influence is for service, not self-glory.

_____
_____
_____

Key Action Step:

One way I will deflect praise back to God or my team is…

_____
_____
_____

Gratitude Moment:

Today, I thank God for reminding me that influence is His gift.

_____
_____
_____

Leadership Win:

Today's humble step in leadership was…

_____
_____
_____

Day 70 – Rest & Reflection

Today's Date: _____

Morning Prayer / Scripture Meditation:

Thank God for trusting you with influence to reflect His heart.

_____

_____

_____

Rest Intention:

Today, I will rest in the truth that God is the ultimate source of influence.

_____

_____

_____

Reflection Highlight:

The most meaningful way I stewarded influence this week was...

_____

_____

_____

Gratitude Moment:

Today, I thank God for three opportunities to influence others this week:

_____

_____

_____

Worship Note / Song / Scripture:

A word, song, or scripture that shaped my use of influence this week was...

_____

_____

_____

END-OF-WEEK WRAP-UP

What area of influence did you grow in this week?

How did you choose faithfulness over ease or comfort?

What fruit came from intentional stewardship?

How will you continue to honor God with your leadership platform?

WEEK 11
Persevering in Purpose

"Let us not become weary in doing good, for at the proper time we will reap a harvest if we do not give up."
— Galatians 6:9 (NIV)

Staying faithful in leadership even when the results are slow and the road is tough.

Perseverance isn't about pushing harder—it's about leaning deeper into God's strength and trusting His timing. Leadership often requires planting seeds that may take months or even years to grow. In those seasons when progress feels slow and results are hidden, it can be tempting to give in to discouragement. But God's Word promises that your labor in Him is never in vain. What feels unseen today is often the foundation for tomorrow's breakthrough.

True perseverance is not fueled by human willpower but by divine grace. When your strength runs low, God renews it. When discouragement whispers "quit," His Spirit breathes fresh courage. Perseverance means choosing to stay rooted in your calling even when the soil feels dry, trusting that God is working in the unseen. It is a daily act of surrender—reminding yourself that the work you do is not for man's approval but for God's glory.

Your perseverance also inspires others. When people watch you endure with faith and integrity, it strengthens their own resolve to remain faithful. Leadership that perseveres teaches that God's promises are worth waiting for, and His harvest always comes at the right time. By refusing to give up, you model resilience, hope, and unwavering trust in God's perfect plan. Your steady commitment becomes a living testimony of what it looks like to lead with endurance anchored in Christ.

REFLECTION QUESTIONS

1. What part of your purpose feels hardest to persevere in right now?

2. How do you stay refreshed in long seasons?

3. What's a past testimony of perseverance that encourages you today?

4. How do you want to show up differently when it gets hard?

WEEKLY ACTION PLAN

This week, I will take one step to remain faithful in my calling by:

_____
_____
_____
_____
_____
_____

A small change I can make to endure with patience and trust in God's timing:

_____
_____
_____
_____
_____
_____

Day 71 – Don't Grow Weary

Today's Date: _____

Morning Prayer / Scripture Meditation:

Read Galatians 6:9. Where are you tempted to grow weary?

_____
_____
_____

Leadership Intention:

Today, I will keep sowing even when I don't yet see the harvest.

_____
_____
_____

Key Action Step:

One area where I will choose persistence is…

_____
_____
_____

Gratitude Moment:

Today, I thank God for sustaining me when…

_____
_____
_____

Leadership Win:

Today's act of perseverance was…

_____
_____
_____

Day 72 – Leaning on God's Strength

Today's Date: _____

Morning Prayer / Scripture Meditation:

Ask God to renew your strength in a weary place.

_____
_____
_____

Leadership Intention:

Today, I will rely on God's strength, not my own.

_____
_____
_____

Key Action Step:

One burden I will release to God today is…

_____
_____
_____

Gratitude Moment:

Today, I thank God for carrying me when I was weak.

_____
_____
_____

Leadership Win:

Today's evidence of God's strength was…

_____
_____
_____

Day 73 – Small Steps Matter

Today's Date: _____

Morning Prayer / Scripture Meditation:

Reflect on how daily obedience builds long-term fruit.

_____
_____
_____

Leadership Intention:

Today, I will be faithful in small things.

_____
_____
_____

Key Action Step:

One small but important task I will complete today is…

_____
_____
_____

Gratitude Moment:

Today, I thank God for progress in little steps.

_____
_____
_____

Leadership Win:

Today's progress through faithfulness was…

_____
_____
_____

Day 74 – Trusting the Timing

Today's Date: _____

Morning Prayer / Scripture Meditation:

Prayerfully thank God that His timing is always right.

Leadership Intention:

Today, I will trust God's timing instead of rushing results.

Key Action Step:

One area I will surrender impatience to God in is…

Gratitude Moment:

Today, I thank God for His perfect timing in…

Leadership Win:

Today's surrender of timing was…

Day 75 – Encouraged to Continue

Today's Date: _____

Morning Prayer / Scripture Meditation:

Ask God to refresh your hope in your purpose.

_____

_____

_____

Leadership Intention:

Today, I will continue even when it's hard.

_____

_____

_____

Key Action Step:

One way I will encourage myself in the Lord today is…

_____

_____

_____

Gratitude Moment:

Today, I thank God for encouragement I received through…

_____

_____

_____

Leadership Win:

Today's encouragement to press on was…

_____

_____

_____

Day 76 – Inspiring Others Through Perseverance

Today's Date: _____

Morning Prayer / Scripture Meditation:

Prayerfully ask God to let your perseverance inspire those you lead.

_____

_____

_____

Leadership Intention:

Today, I will model faithfulness for others.

_____

_____

_____

Key Action Step:

One way I will show perseverance to my team/family is…

_____

_____

_____

Gratitude Moment:

Today, I thank God for leaders who showed me endurance.

_____

_____

_____

Leadership Win:

Today's example of perseverance was…

_____

_____

_____

Day 77 – Rest & Reflection

Today's Date: _____

Morning Prayer / Scripture Meditation:

Thank God for strengthening you to stay the course.

_____

_____

_____

Rest Intention:

Today, I will rest in God's promise that the harvest will come.

_____

_____

_____

Reflection Highlight:

The most meaningful area I persevered in this week was…

_____

_____

_____

Gratitude Moment:

Today, I thank God for three ways He helped me endure this week:

_____

_____

_____

Worship Note / Song / Scripture

A word, song, or scripture that helped me persevere this week was…

_____

_____

_____

END-OF-WEEK WRAP-UP

Where did you feel most strengthened to persevere this week?

What progress—big or small—are you celebrating?

How did God encourage or surprise you through the process?

What will you carry forward into the next stage of your purpose journey?

WEEK 12
Leading with Hope

> *"But those who hope in the LORD will renew their strength. They will soar on wings like eagles; they will run and not grow weary, they will walk and not be faint."*
> — Isaiah 40:31 (NIV)

Infusing hope into your leadership, renewing strength in God, and inspiring others with a forward-looking vision.

Hope is more than wishful thinking—it's the confident expectation that God will fulfill His promises. As leaders, hope is the fuel that keeps us moving forward when results seem delayed or obstacles appear overwhelming. When we lead with hope, we don't ignore reality—we acknowledge it, but we choose to see it through the lens of God's faithfulness. Hope steadies us, reminding us that no season is wasted and that renewal always comes for those who wait on the Lord.

Leadership rooted in hope also strengthens those around us. People follow leaders who carry a hopeful perspective, especially in times of uncertainty. When you lead with hope, you become a source of courage for others. Your faith in God's promises and your ability to speak encouragement breathe life into weary hearts. A hopeful leader doesn't just keep themselves moving forward—they pull others forward too.

Finally, hope keeps vision alive. It allows you to see beyond temporary setbacks and hold on to God's bigger picture. Without hope, leadership becomes heavy, discouraging, and short-sighted. But with hope, even small steps take on eternal significance. As you lead this week, ask God to renew your strength through hope, to anchor your heart in His promises, and to help you reflect that hope to those entrusted to your care.

REFLECTION QUESTIONS

1. What growth have you seen in your leadership over the past 90 days?

2. How do you stay refreshed in long seasons?

3. What breakthrough moment, scripture, or lesson stands out most?

4. How have you grown in purpose, joy, and spiritual maturity?

5. What is God calling you to do or become in this next season?

WEEKLY ACTION PLAN

This week, I will take one step to renew my hope in the Lord by:

_____
_____
_____
_____
_____
_____

A small change I can make to encourage others with hope this week:

_____
_____
_____
_____
_____
_____

Day 78 – Hope Anchors the Soul

Today's Date: _____

Morning Prayer / Scripture Meditation:

Read Isaiah 40:31. Where do you need God to renew your strength today?

_____

_____

_____

Leadership Intention:

Today, I will let hope steady my spirit.

_____

_____

_____

Key Action Step:

One area I will anchor in hope is…

_____

_____

_____

Gratitude Moment:

Today, I thank God for His unfailing promises.

_____

_____

_____

Leadership Win:

Today's evidence of renewed hope was…

_____

_____

_____

Day 79 – Hope in Hard Places

Today's Date: _____

Morning Prayer / Scripture Meditation:

Ask God to remind you of His faithfulness in difficulty.

_____
_____
_____

Leadership Intention:

Today, I will choose hope in the face of challenges.

_____
_____
_____

Key Action Step:

One difficulty I will approach with hope is…

_____
_____
_____

Gratitude Moment:

Today, I thank God for never leaving me in my struggles.

_____
_____
_____

Leadership Win:

Today's moment of strength through hope was…

_____
_____
_____

Day 80 – Leading with Expectation

Today's Date: _____

Morning Prayer / Scripture Meditation:

Prayerfully expect God to move as you lead today.

_____

_____

_____

Leadership Intention:

Today, I will lead with anticipation of God's goodness.

_____

_____

_____

Key Action Step:

One area where I need God's grace to finish strong is…

_____

_____

_____

Gratitude Moment:

Today, I thank God for blessings yet to come.

_____

_____

_____

Leadership Win:

Today's hopeful decision was…

_____

_____

_____

Day 81 – Hope for Others

Today's Date: _____

Morning Prayer / Scripture Meditation:

Ask God to use you to speak hope into someone's life.

_____
_____
_____

Leadership Intention:

Today, I will be a voice of encouragement and hope.

_____
_____
_____

Key Action Step:

One person I will encourage with hope today is…

_____
_____
_____

Gratitude Moment:

Today, I thank God for people who spoke hope over me.

_____
_____
_____

Leadership Win:

Today's impact through encouragement was…

_____
_____
_____

Day 82 – Hope Renews Strength

Today's Date: _____

Morning Prayer / Scripture Meditation:

Reflect on how hope restores your energy and perseverance.

_____

_____

_____

Leadership Intention:

Today, I will lean on God to renew my strength.

_____

_____

_____

Key Action Step:

One way I will rest in God to gain strength is…

_____

_____

_____

Gratitude Moment:

Today, I thank God for restoring me when…

_____

_____

_____

Leadership Win:

Today's renewal in strength was…

_____

_____

_____

Day 83 – Hope-Fueled Vision

Today's Date: _____

Morning Prayer / Scripture Meditation:

Ask God to give you a hopeful perspective for the future.

_____
_____
_____

Leadership Intention:

Today, I will see my leadership through the lens of hope by…

_____
_____
_____

Key Action Step:

One area where I will cast vision rooted in hope is…

_____
_____
_____

Gratitude Moment:

Today, I thank God for hope that never fails.

_____
_____
_____

Leadership Win:

Today's hopeful vision step was…

_____
_____
_____

Day 84 – Rest & Reflection

Today's Date: _____

Morning Prayer / Scripture Meditation:

Thank God for renewing your hope this week.

___

Rest Intention:

Today, I will rest in the certainty of God's promises.

___

Reflection Highlight:

The most important way hope shaped my leadership this week was…

___

Gratitude Moment:

Today, I thank God for three ways He renewed my hope this week:

___

Worship Note / Song / Scripture

A word, song, or scripture that lifted my hope this week was…

___

END-OF-WEEK WRAP-UP

This week, I experienced hope through…

_____
_____
_____
_____

One challenge I faced and how God gave me strength was…

_____
_____
_____
_____

A person I encouraged with hope this week was…

_____
_____
_____
_____

What was greatest lesson God taught me about hope?

_____
_____
_____
_____

WEEK 13
Finishing Faithfully

"I have fought the good fight, I have finished the race, I have kept the faith."
— 2 Timothy 4:7 (NIV)

Ending strong, honoring the journey, and committing to the next step with God.

Faithful leadership isn't just about how you start—it's about how you finish. Starting something new can be exciting, but finishing with integrity requires endurance, focus, and grace. Paul's words remind us that leadership is not a sprint; it is a lifelong race marked by seasons of trial, growth, and victory. To finish faithfully means staying true to your calling and keeping your eyes fixed on Jesus, even when the path gets hard.

As you complete this 90-day journey, reflect on the growth you've experienced and the grace that carried you. Every step, whether uphill or smooth, has shaped your leadership and strengthened your faith. Finishing faithfully means pausing to thank God for His provision, acknowledging the lessons learned, and celebrating the progress made. Gratitude fuels perseverance, and reflection prepares you for the next assignment God places before you.

Finishing well also means looking forward with renewed commitment. Leadership doesn't end with one season—it continues as God opens new doors and expands your influence. A faithful finish in one chapter becomes a strong foundation for the next. As you step forward, carry with you the wisdom gained, the faith refined, and the vision clarified. Trust that the same God who has brought you this far will continue to guide, equip, and strengthen you for every race ahead.

REFLECTION QUESTIONS

1. What growth have you seen in your leadership over the past 90 days?

2. How do you stay refreshed in long seasons?

3. What breakthrough moment, scripture, or lesson stands out most?

4. How have you grown in purpose, joy, and spiritual maturity?

5. What is God calling you to do or become in this next season?

WEEKLY ACTION PLAN

This week, I will take one step to honor God as I finish this journey well by:

_____
_____
_____
_____
_____
_____

A small change I can make to prepare for my next season with faith:

_____
_____
_____
_____
_____
_____

Day 85 – Running the Race

Today's Date: _____

Morning Prayer / Scripture Meditation:

Read 2 Timothy 4:7. What race has God called you to run faithfully?

_____
_____
_____

Leadership Intention:

Today, I will stay committed to the race God set before me.

_____
_____
_____

Key Action Step:

One way I will keep running with endurance today is…

_____
_____
_____

Gratitude Moment:

Today, I thank God for sustaining me on this journey.

_____
_____
_____

Leadership Win:

Today's step of faithfulness was…

_____
_____
_____

Day 86 – Honoring the Journey

Today's Date: _____

Morning Prayer / Scripture Meditation:

Reflect on how far God has brought you in this season.

_____
_____
_____

Leadership Intention:

Today, I will celebrate progress, not perfection.

_____
_____
_____

Key Action Step:

One lesson from this journey I will carry forward is…

_____
_____
_____

Gratitude Moment:

Today, I thank God for His grace through each step.

_____
_____
_____

Leadership Win:

Today's reflection on growth was…

_____
_____
_____

Day 87 – Grace to Finish Strong

Today's Date: _____

Morning Prayer / Scripture Meditation:

Prayerfully ask God for strength and grace to finish well.

_____

_____

_____

Leadership Intention:

Today, I will lean on God's grace to endure.

_____

_____

_____

Key Action Step:

One area where I need God's grace to finish strong is…

_____

_____

_____

Gratitude Moment:

Today, I thank God for His sustaining grace.

_____

_____

_____

Leadership Win:

Today's faithful moment was…

_____

_____

_____

Day 88 – Passing the Baton

Today's Date: _____

Morning Prayer / Scripture Meditation:

Consider who you are preparing to carry the work forward.

_____
_____
_____

Leadership Intention:

Today, I will invest in the next generation.

_____
_____
_____

Key Action Step:

One way I can pour into someone else this week is…

_____
_____
_____

Gratitude Moment:

Today, I thank God for those who paved the way for me.

_____
_____
_____

Leadership Win:

Today's legacy-building step was…

_____
_____
_____

Day 89 – Finishing with Faith

Today's Date: _____

Morning Prayer / Scripture Meditation:

Reflect on what it means to keep the faith until the end.

_____

_____

_____

Leadership Intention:

Today, I will guard my faith as my greatest treasure.

_____

_____

_____

Key Action Step:

One way I will strengthen my faith today is…

_____

_____

_____

Gratitude Moment:

Today, I thank God for keeping me strong in faith through …

_____

_____

_____

Leadership Win:

Today's victory of faith was…

_____

_____

_____

Day 90 – Rest & Reflection

Today's Date: _____

Morning Prayer / Scripture Meditation:
Thank God for carrying you through these 90 days.

_____
_____
_____

Rest Intention:
Today, I will rest in the assurance that God finishes what He starts.

_____
_____
_____

Reflection Highlight:
The most important lesson I will carry from this 90 day journey is…

_____
_____
_____

Gratitude Moment:
Today, I thank God for three ways He transformed me in this season:

_____
_____
_____

Worship Note / Song / Scripture:
A word, song, or scripture that marked this season for me was…

_____
_____
_____

END-OF-WEEK WRAP-UP

What transformation are you celebrating as you finish this journal?

_____

_____

_____

_____

What prayer or declaration will you carry forward?

_____

_____

_____

_____

How has God prepared your heart to lead in new ways?

_____

_____

_____

_____

What will "faithful leadership" look like for you going forward?

_____

_____

_____

_____

CLOSING REFLECTION

As you finish this 90-day journey, pause and take a deep breath of gratitude. You have spent intentional time growing in faith, leadership, and purpose. This journal was never meant to be just pages of words, but a journey of transformation. You have prayed through challenges, sought wisdom, wrestled with courage, and embraced the truth that leadership is not about titles but about serving, stewarding, and finishing faithfully.

Take a moment to look back at the weeks behind you. Where have you seen growth in your heart, habits, and leadership? What new revelations has the Lord stirred in you? How has He met you in the quiet, strengthened you in the hard places, and reminded you of your unique calling? Reflecting on these moments helps you recognize that leadership is not a destination but a lifelong walk with Jesus.

And now, look ahead. God is not finished with you. This is only the beginning of deeper faith, greater influence, and new opportunities to lead with courage and humility. Carry forward the truths you've written, the prayers you've prayed, and the vision God has placed within you. Lead with open hands, surrendered heart, and steadfast spirit, knowing that the One who has called you is faithful to complete the good work He began in you.

> "The measure of a life, after all, is not its duration, but its donation."
>
> — Corrie Ten Boom

PRAYER OF COMMISSION

Heavenly Father,

I thank You for the journey You have led me on over these past 90 days. Thank You for every lesson, every challenge, and every moment of grace that has shaped me into a leader after Your heart. I acknowledge that leadership is not mine to own but mine to steward, and I commit all that I am and all that I do into Your hands.

Lord, fill me with courage to walk by faith, wisdom to lead with discernment, and humility to serve with compassion. Guard my heart with integrity, strengthen me with perseverance, and empower me to finish faithfully every assignment You entrust to me. May my leadership reflect Your love, bring glory to Your name, and make an eternal impact in the lives of others.

I step forward today, commissioned by Your Spirit, confident that You go before me, walk beside me, and live within me. My leadership belongs to You. Use me, Lord, for Your Kingdom and for Your glory.

In Jesus' name, Amen.

KEEP GROWING WITH THE TRIPLE JOY GROUP & OLIVE JOY MINISTRIES

At the Triple Joy Group, we are committed to equipping leaders like you to grow, lead, and live with joy and purpose. Now that you've completed the 90-day journey, here are resources to support your continued growth and impact:

Maxwell DISC Personality Assessment

Gain powerful insight into your communication style, leadership approach, and relational dynamics.
- Personalized DISC report
- Actionable growth tips
- Optional debrief with a certified DISC coach
- Great for individuals, couples, teams, and organizations

Learn more at www.triplejoygroup.com

Leadership Coaching

Ready to elevate your leadership journey?
Partner with a certified coach for:
- Clarity in purpose and direction
- Strategies for influence and impact
- Growth in confidence, focus, and follow-through

Packages available on 8-week tracks.

Workshops & Trainings

Bring a transformational learning experience to your organization or team. Topics include:
- Purpose-Driven Leadership
- Emotional Intelligence & Self-Awareness
- Leading with Joy
- DISC Communication & Team Dynamics

Available for corporate, nonprofit, and faith-based settings.

Let's Stay Connected

Olive Joy Ministries
- Website: www.olivejoyministries.com
- Email: info@olivejoyministries.com
- Facebook: Patricia Akinrogunde (Olive Joy Ministries)

The Triple Joy Group
- Website: www.triplejoygroup.com
- Email: admin@triplejoygroup.com
- Instagram: Triple Joy Group
- Facebook: Triple Joy Group

Leadership is a lifestyle—and you don't have to grow alone.

Take your next step with the Triple Joy Group.

We're here to help you rise with purpose and lead with joy.

Are you a journal lover? Keep an eye out for other journals coming soon!

- The Triple Joy Financial Journal
- The Triple Joy Relationship Journal
- The Triple Joy Relationship Journal (Couples Edition)

ABOUT THE AUTHOR

Dr. Patricia Akinrogunde is a faith-filled leader, certified Executive, Relationship, and Wellness Coach, and a member of the Maxwell Leadership Certified Team. She combines her deep love for God with over 20 years of leadership experience across the military, federal government, and ministry, guiding others to lead with conviction, compassion, and purpose.

As the founder of Olive Joy Ministries, and Chief Execute Officer of The Triple Joy Group, Patricia empowers believers to grow in their identity, deepen their relationship with God, and lead boldly in every area of life—whether at home, in the workplace, or in ministry. Her journey from a once-quiet child to a confident voice in leadership is a testimony of God's grace, healing, and calling.

With a Doctorate in Community Care and Counseling, multiple master's degrees, and extensive experience as a speaker, professor, and trainer, Patricia brings both spiritual depth and practical insight to her work.

Patricia resides in Maryland with her husband, Sunday, and her three children, Olivia, Hannah, and Sarah. Other books by Patricia include The Triple Joy Leadership Journal, The Triple Joy Relationship Journal, and The Triple Joy Financial Journal. You can follow Patricia and all her creative content on Instagram @TripleJoyGroup.

> "For we are God's masterpiece. He has created us anew in Christ Jesus, so we can do the good things He planned for us long ago."
> – Ephesians 2:10 (NLT)

www.ingramcontent.com/pod-product-compliance
Lightning Source LLC
Chambersburg PA
CBHW041135130526
44582CB00029B/117